# THE MOON EXPLORER Guide

WILLIAM THOMSON

**Imray**

**William Thomson FRGS is an author, artist and adventurer.**

He is founder of *Tide School* and a Fellow of the Royal Geographical Society. William is author and illustrator of *The Book of Tides* and *The World of Tides*, and regularly writes for magazines including Yachting Monthly, Coast, Outdoor Swimmer and Sailing Today.

William lives full-time aboard his yellow catamaran *Luna* with his partner Naomi, their children Ottilie and Arva, and the family's rescued Mallard duck 'Herby'. The crew are currently on a long-term circumnavigation, taking time to fully explore the places they visit while William writes and runs his *Tide School,* teaching people how to 'Seas The Power'.

In addition to sailing, William is a trained PADI Rescue Diver, sea swimmer and surfer. This multi-dimensional approach to adventures brings a practical experience to William's work, which is shared through this series of Explorer Guides - made for anyone who enjoys the sea.

Published by
Imray, Laurie, Norie and Wilson Ltd
Wych House
The Broadway
St Ives
Cambridgeshire
PE27 5BT

+44 (0) 1480 462114
ilnw@imray.com
2021

© William Thomson, 2021

All rights reserved. No part of this publication may be reproduced, transmitted or used in any form by any means, electronic or mechanical, including photocopy, recording or anyinformation storage and retrieval systems, without permission in writing from the Publisher.

British Library Cataloguing in Publication Data.
A catalogue record for this title is available from the British Library.

ISBN 978 178679 296 9

Printed and bound in Croatia by Denona

| | | |
|---|---|---|
| 6 | INTRODUCTION | |
| 12 | CHANGES WITH **TIME** | |
| 26 | MOON **PHASES** | |
| 38 | **CLUES** FOR EXPLORERS | |
| 48 | **PHENOMENA** MADE BY THE MOON | |
| 54 | LUNAR DICTIONARY | |

We live in a fascinating age of information where accurate forecasts streamed to our phones can tell us exactly what the winds, waves, tides and streams will be doing every hour of the coming days. But what these forecasts do not tell us is how these conditions interact with each other and the coast to create a specific sea state at a certain time and place. The purpose of this series is to fill that gap, equipping you with the skill to take a forecast and use that knowledge to predict what to expect, where and when.

Why is this important? Because if you know what is going to happen in an hour around the headland, or tomorrow in the bay, you will be better informed to make decisions that enhance your safety and performance. Those hidden dangers lurking beneath the surface will be less of a threat because you were aware of them long in advance, while precious windows of opportunity will always be made best use of. In short, with these guides at your side you will be one step closer to being in the right place at the right time, safely bypassing the wrong places at the wrong times.

To the untrained eye, the sea can seem like a chaotic environment, puzzling and unpredictable. But with guidance, a natural order appears from the chaos. There is always an explanation for why something is happening, and it is usually a blend of simple factors coinciding - the shape of coastline, time of day, weather conditions, moon phase. In this collection of books we will explore all these factors one at a time, analysing their individual effect on the sea's moods. To achieve this, each guide focuses on a different element (Tides, Streams, The Moon, Winds, Waves, Rips, Clouds, Currents, Stars) with this book organised into two main sections; 'Changes with Time' and 'Moon Phases', with each page analysing the effects of a single variable.

Infographics are an integral role in this work because they are so effective at helping to explain concepts. But when it comes to cycles, such as the moon orbiting the earth or tide waves spinning around oceans, a stationary image can only show one moment in the cycle and you need to visualise the rest. This can be difficult, so to make learning easier there is a collection of DIY models to accompany these guides. The idea is for you to download the designs for free at www.tidalcompass.com using the code EXPLORERGUIDES and assemble the models at home, using them alongside these pages to better understand natural processes.

▶

If you are reading this book you are aware of the sea's power. Although we can train our bodies to be as strong as possible, in a strength contest with the ocean we will lose every time. Even the strongest boats may be overwhelmed by a rogue wave. But luckily we have a secret weapon - the power of our minds. Instead of trying to achieve our objectives with brawn, we can use our brains. These guides will help you to do this by deepening your understanding of nature's forces and sharing ways to harness this energy to your advantage, going further and faster while consuming less of your own precious energy. If our ultimate goal is to be summed up in three words, it must surely be 'Seas The Power'.

**William Thomson**
Aboard *Luna*, at sea

# TIDE
## SCHOOL

Join Tide School to boost your knowledge
www.tide-school.com

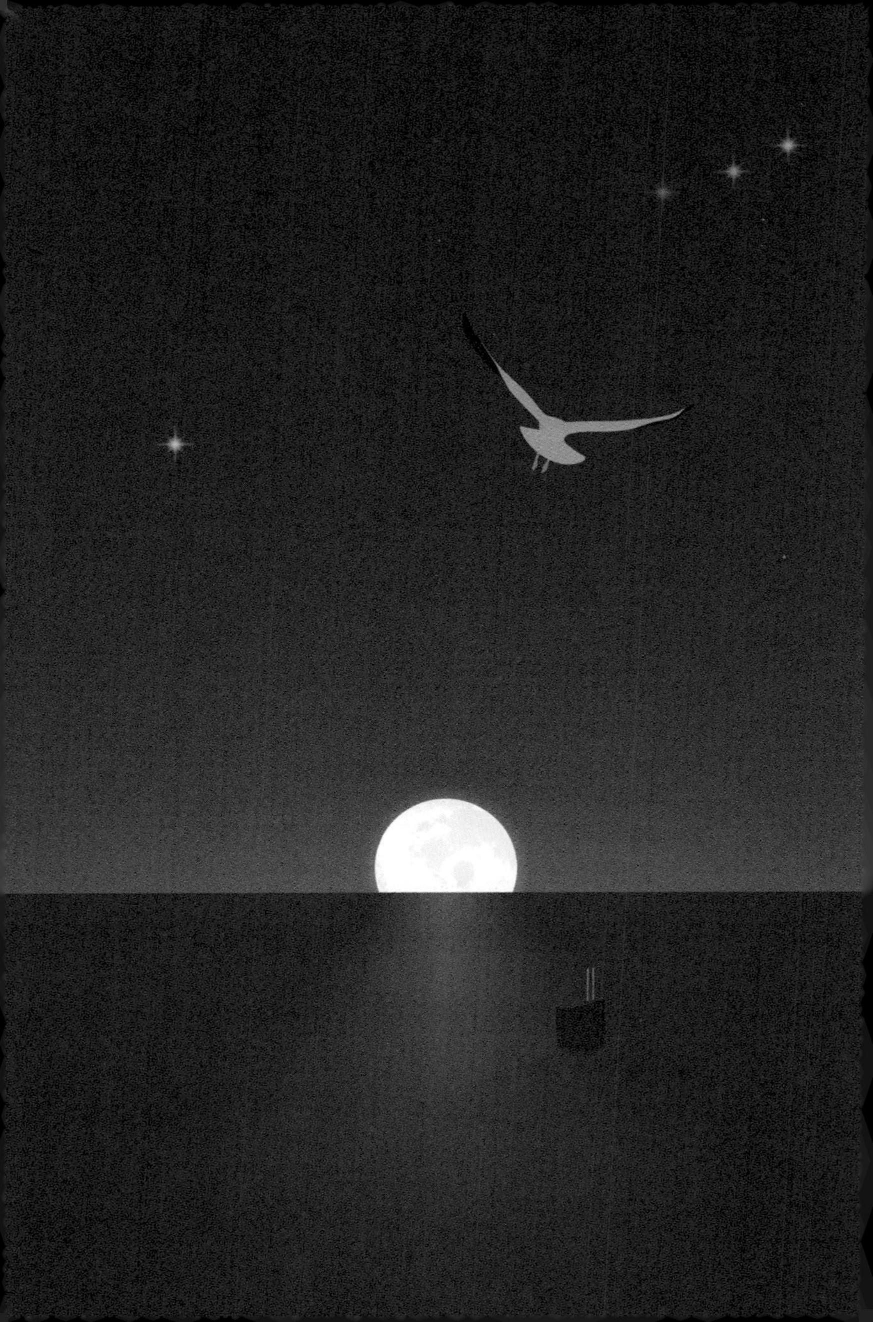

**Once a month the moon orbits the earth and this determines where it is in the sky and what the tides are doing.**

In 'the big splash' theory of how the moon was made, a mars-sized astronomical body crashed into earth 4.5 billion years ago, knocking our planet over by 23.5 degrees and resulting in the moon forming from the debris. Since that dramatic event, the moon has excelled at elusiveness; it appears in different places at different times, always a slightly different shape, tilted ever so slightly one way or the other. It is both familiar and unknown, close enough for humans to reach but far enough away to create a sense of awe at the scale of our universe.

Despite our fascination with the moon, very few understand its movements, like why it sometimes rises in the daytime or why it changes shape from one day to the next. Then there is its effect on the tides. In this Explorer Guide you will learn all these things, plus more; you will be able to predict the tides with a single glance at the moon, and with that quick look you will also be able to get your bearings - day or night - instantly knowing which way you are facing while navigating through the ever-changing environment shaped by the gravitational pull from the moon.

## CHANGES WITH
# TIME

As the earth spins on its axis and the moon orbits the earth you will notice hourly, daily and weekly changes in how the moon looks and where it is in the sky. These changes have a profound impact on the tide times and intensity while also determining which nights experience moonlight.

**In this section we will explore the simple cycles that make these changes in the moon throughout a day, week, month and year.**

## THE MOON MOVES
>>> **15 DEGREES WEST EVERY HOUR** >>>

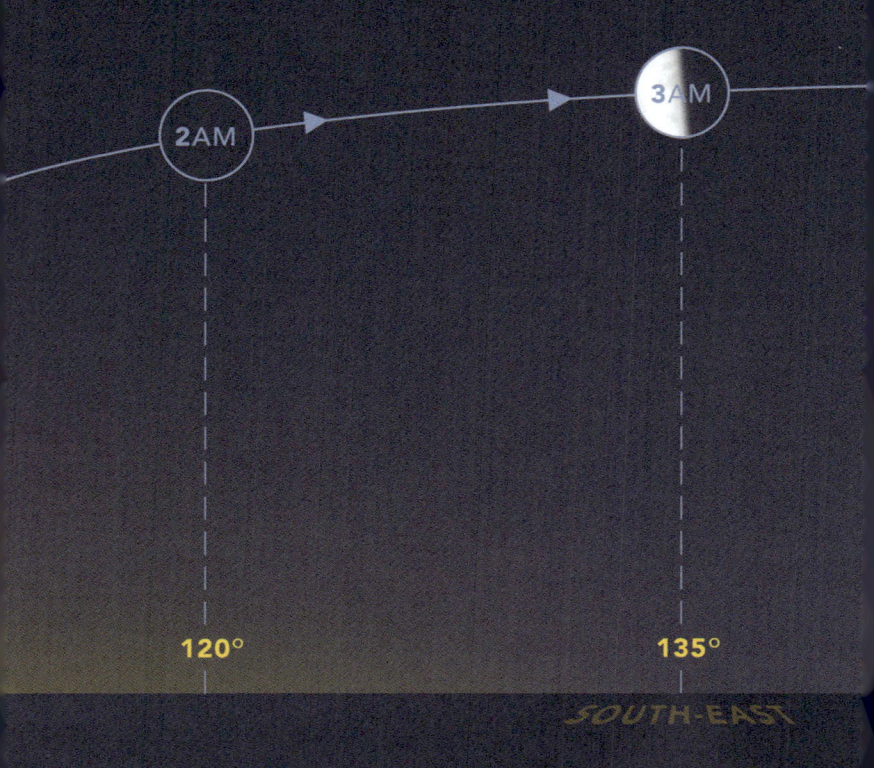

2AM

3AM

120°

135°

*SOUTH-EAST*

## The moon moves 15 degrees through the sky every hour

If you observe the moon over a period of several hours you will notice it moves through the sky from the east towards the west, passing due south when it is highest in the sky (if the moon's declination is south of your latitude - *see page 22*). Although the moon does move around the earth once a month, this hourly passage across our horizon is actually made by the earth spinning on its axis, creating the illusion of the moon moving. Because the earth makes a 360-degree spin every 24 hours, this equates to 15 degrees per hour, which is why celestial bodies like the moon, planets, sun and stars move 15 degrees through the sky every hour.

Because the earth spins counter-clockwise on its axis, the effect is that celestial bodies move westwards in the sky, or from left to right in the northern hemisphere (and right to left in the southern hemisphere). Understanding this concept is useful when exploring because it makes sense of where to expect the moon, especially if you last saw it a couple of hours ago. This is particularly helpful in the daytime when only a sliver (crescent) is visible because it does not stand out as much as the Full Moon at night.

# PERIGEE

APOGEE

=

# APOGEE

=

## The moon looks biggest once a month

In the *Tides Explorer Guide* we learnt how the moon exerts a stronger gravitational pull when it is closer to earth around once a month, a consequence of it having an elliptical (egg shaped) orbit around earth. When the moon is closest we call it perigee (peri = close / gee = earth) and it is 356,500km away. In contrast, when the moon is at the furthest point in its orbit, at 406,700 km away, we call it apogee (apo = far / gee = earth). The difference between these occasions is that the moon looks 15% bigger and 30% brighter at perigee.

If you see a Full Moon that is especially large then expect strong 'perigean spring tides', colloquially named 'super tides'. In contrast, a small half moon signifies apogee at the same time as neap tides, so there will particularly weak tides called 'apogean neap tides'. However, bear in mind that when the moon is low on the horizon it looks bigger than when it is high in the sky, a phenomena known as 'The Moon Illusion' that has baffled astronomers since ancient times. A simple way to test this is to find a pebble the size of the moon when held at arms length and see if they remain the same size as the moon rises.

**FIRST QUARTER**

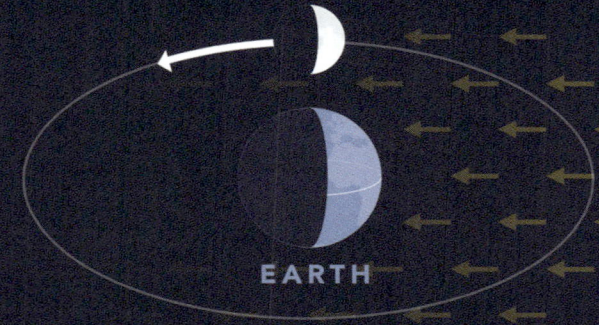

EARTH

SUN

## The moon's face changes every day

The moon does not create its own light. Instead, it reflects the sun's light onto earth. At the Full Moon the whole face is lit up because we are looking at the side facing the sun. But a fortnight later at the New Moon we cannot see any of the side lit up because it is facing away from us, which is why the moon appears dark in the sky. For the weeks in between, half the moon's face is visible because it is at right angles to the sun and us; when the right side is lit the moon is 'waxing' and when the left side is illuminated it is 'waning'. For a visual demonstration of how this works, see the experiment at the beginning of the Moon Phases chapter.

Being able to quickly look at the moon and work out its position on the monthly orbit is an incredibly valuable skill. For example, if you are in the northern hemisphere and the right half is illuminated it must be a First Quarter phase, with its position in relation to the sun and earth shown in the diagram. Using this knowledge you can deduce that neap tides will be in around 2 days and if you remember your local high tide time at Full Moon you can even work out today's tide times by subtracting 6 hours from that time (we look at this in more detail in the *Tides Explorer Guide*).

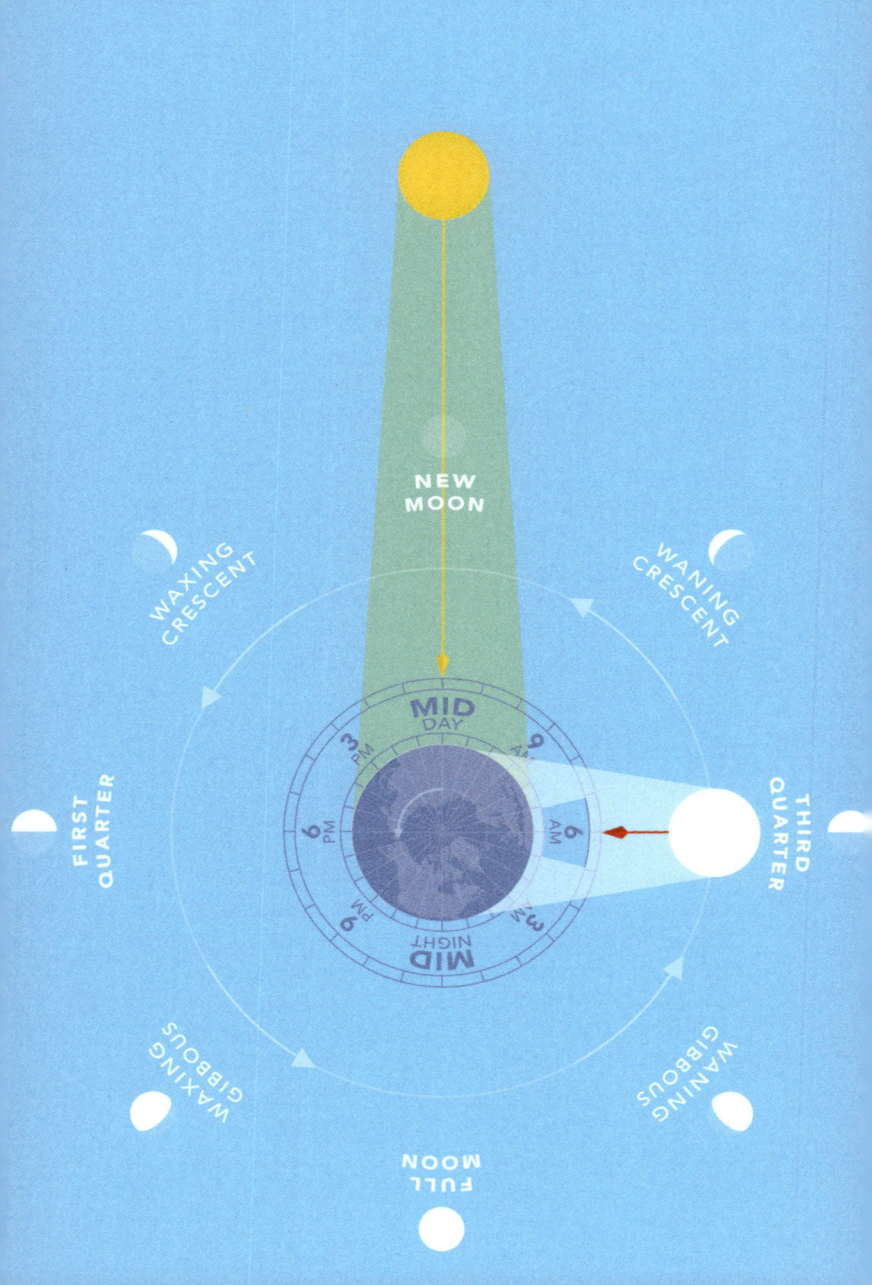

NEW MOON

WAXING CRESCENT

WANING CRESCENT

FIRST QUARTER

THIRD QUARTER

MID DAY

MID NIGHT

WAXING GIBBOUS

WANING GIBBOUS

FULL MOON

## The moon is highest in the sky 50 minutes later every day

As the earth spins on its axis, the moon appears to rise and fall in the sky. When your meridian (an imaginary line running from north pole to south pole, passing through your position) lines up with the moon, it will be highest in the sky for that day and we call this moment 'culmination'. The sun always culminates every 24 hours around midday, but the moon culminates 50 minutes later every day because in the time your meridian has made a 360-degree spin, the moon has moved 12 degrees in its monthly orbit of earth and it takes another 50 minutes to realign.

By knowing the moon's position in relation to the sun and earth you can predict the time of day it will be highest. For example, the Third Quarter phase (shown in the illustration opposite) is highest at 6am because this is when your meridian lines up with the moon. This takes a lot of visualisation, so to make life easier you can download, print and assemble the model opposite from www.tidalcompass.com. By moving the moon to any phase and then spinning the earth on its axis, you can clearly see the time of day your meridian lines up with the moon throughout the lunar month.

# CELESTIAL SPHERE

**NORTH CELESTIAL POLE**

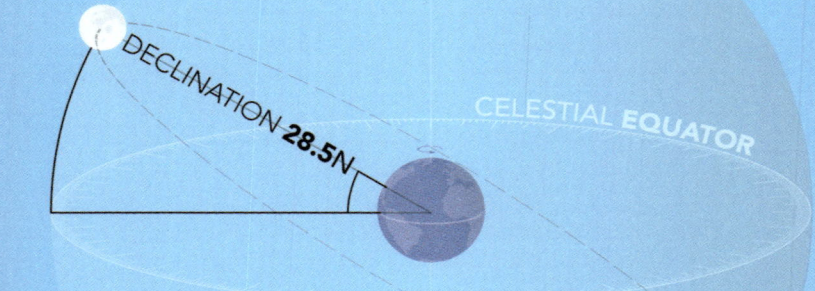

DECLINATION 28.5N

CELESTIAL **EQUATOR**

MOON'S ORBIT

**SOUTH CELESTIAL POLE**

### An important term to understand is 'declination'

To simplify astronomy we imagine all celestial bodies (the moon, stars, planets and the sun) set on a 'Celestial Sphere' projected out from the earth, with its equator and poles aligned with ours. To pinpoint the moon's vertical position on this sphere we use the term *declination*, which is measured up to 90 degrees north or south of the equator, just like latitude on earth. Because the two 'balls' of earth and the celestial sphere are aligned, when the moon has the same declination as your latitude, it will be directly overhead when it culminates at the moment your meridians align.

This means that when the moon is at the highest point of its orbit with a declination of 28.5 degrees north, it will culminate directly overhead places with latitude of 28.5 degrees north, such as the Canary Islands. But for every degree difference between your latitude and the moon's declination, it will be one degree lower above the horizon at 'culmination'. Crucially, if your latitude is further north than the moon's declination it will culminate due south, but if your latitude is further south than the moon's declination, it will culminate due north.

**NORTH CELESTIAL POLE**

**NORTHERLY DECLINATION**

A

SUN

B

**SOUTHERLY DECLINATION**

**SOUTH CELESTIAL POLE**

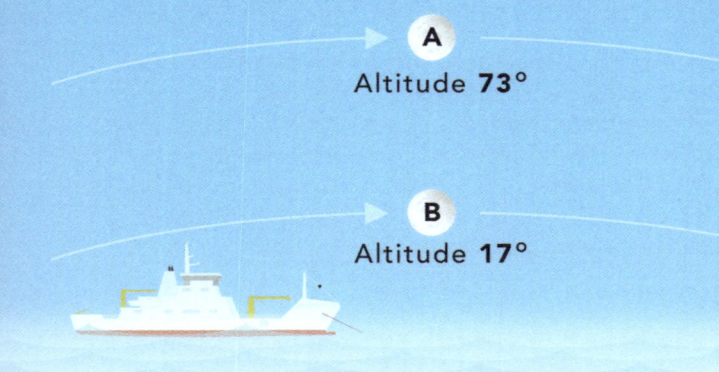

A
Altitude **73°**

B
Altitude **17°**

VIEWED FROM LATITUDE 45 DEGREES NORTH

## The moon rises to a different height every day

Because the moon's orbit is not aligned with our equator, its declination constantly changes and this results in the moon rising to a different height every day. The first mismatch in orbits is a 5-degree tilt of the moon on a plane between the centre of the sun and the centre of earth. On top of this, the earth's 23.5-degree tilt from 'The Big Splash' results in the moon's declination ranging from 28.5 degrees north at the 'top' of its orbit (Position A) to 28.5 degrees south at the 'bottom' of its orbit (Position B).

If you know your latitude and the moon's declination, calculating the *angular distance* between the two and subtracting that number from 90 will tell you the height the moon will culminate (be highest in the sky). For example, if your latitude is 45 degrees north and the moon's declination is 28 degrees north, the *angular distance* is 17 (45-28 = 17) so its altitude at culmination will be 73 degrees above the horizon (90-17=73). Furthermore, the higher the moon's declination, the longer it will be in the sky; as a general rule, a 15-degree rise in declination makes the moon rise an hour earlier and set an hour later.

MOON
# PHASES

As the moon orbits the earth it has four main moon phases; the New Moon, First Quarter, Full Moon and Third Quarter. Each one looks different, rises and sets at a specific time of day and directly affects the tide times and intensity.

**In this section you will learn what to expect from each of the main moon phases and how to make the most of their quirks when you plan your adventures.**

# MOON PHASE **EXPERIMENT**

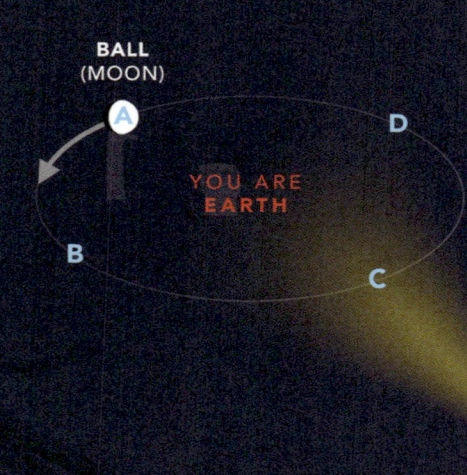

**BALL (MOON)**

A

YOU ARE EARTH

D

B

C

TORCH (SUN)

| A | B | C | D |
|---|---|---|---|
| **FULL** MOON | **THIRD** QUARTER | **NEW** MOON | **FIRST** QUARTER |

**To better understand moon phases, try this experiment; all you need is a torch and a ball.**

Step 1: Set the torch in the corner of a room facing into the middle. Turn off the lights and stand in the middle of the room, holding the ball up so that it is directly ahead of you. The torch represents the sun, the ball is the moon and you are earth.

Step 2: Stand with your back to the torch so the whole ball is lit up. This is the Full Moon and Position A in the diagram. Now make a ninety-degree turn to the left so the left half of the ball is lit. This movement represents a week's orbit of the moon and the new position is 'Third Quarter' at Position B.

Step 3: Do another quarter turn so you are facing directly at the torch. This is the New Moon and the side of the ball lit up is facing the torch, so it appears dark.

Step 4: Do a continuous 360-degree turn, stopping when you get back to the New Moon. This represents a lunar month and you will see how the lit part of the moon's face changes as you move around, growing in size (waxing) from the New Moon to Full Moon and then waning as it approaches the New Moon.

# MOON PHASE
# NEW MOON

**WANING CRESCENT** → → **WAXING CRESCENT**

**TIDE INTENSITY**

MIN. — NEAPS    MAX. — SPRINGS

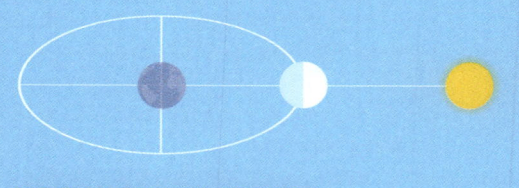

**POSITION IN ORBIT**

E — 6AM    W — 6PM

**MOONRISE & MOONSET**
(APPROXIMATE)

## The New Moon is the beginning of a lunar month

Every lunar month starts with the New Moon and although this sounds exciting, there is not a huge amount to look at because the lit side of the moon is facing away from us (a result of the New Moon being directly between the sun and earth). Added to this, when a sliver of the illuminated side can be seen on the days around a New Moon, it rises in the morning and sets in the evening so gets drowned out by the bright daylight. Thankfully, there is one advantage of this phase; it creates dark nights that are perfect for stargazing because the lack of moonlight means faint stars stand out more.

Despite a weak visual appearance from the moon, it makes up for it with strong tides. Because the New Moon is directly aligned with the sun and earth, the combined gravitational forces on our seas are enhanced and we experience strong spring tides with higher highs, lower lows, faster tidal streams and shorter periods of slack water. Contrary to popular belief, the name comes from the tide 'springing forward' and spring tides have nothing to do with the season of spring; they happen every fortnight, approximately 2 days after the New Moon and Full Moon.

# MOON PHASE
# FIRST QUARTER

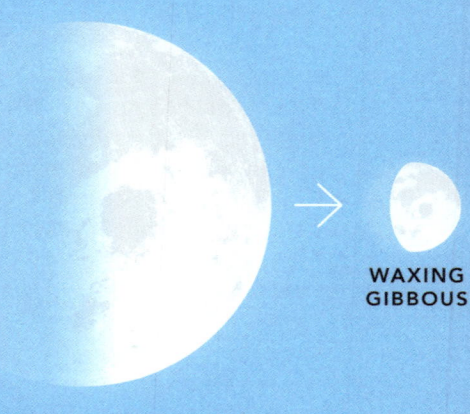

WAXING CRESCENT → WAXING GIBBOUS

**TIDE INTENSITY** — MIN. NEAPS — MAX. SPRINGS

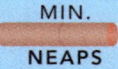

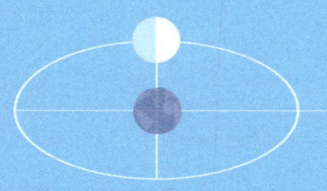

**POSITION IN ORBIT**

**MOONRISE & MOONSET**
(APPROXIMATE)

E — MID DAY
W — MID NIGHT

## The First Quarter phase happens when the right half is lit

The first quarter phase happens a week after the New Moon, when the moon has completed the first quarter of its monthly orbit around earth, hence the name. Because the moon has a counter-clockwise orbit of the earth, when looking at a plan view of the North Pole the First Quarter is exactly ninety degrees to the right of a line drawn through the sun and earth. This means the sun's rays bathe the right half of the moon in light, the reason it is sometimes called the 'First Half' moon. Regardless of whether you call it 'half' or 'quarter', the 'first' part helps remember that it lights up the first part of the night.

As a general rule, the First Quarter rises around mid-day, is highest in the sky around 6pm and then sets around midnight. This means that if you are planning an adventure that extends into the early evening, timing it for this moon phase will help because the moonlight will guide you for a few hours after the sun sets. Another advantage of this time is the weak 'neap' tides; because the moon is at right angles to the sun and earth, the combined gravitational pull on our seas is less and tides are mellow with reduced tidal ranges and slower tidal streams.

# MOON PHASE
# FULL MOON

WAXING GIBBOUS → → WANING GIBBOUS

**TIDE INTENSITY** — MIN. NEAPS — MAX. SPRINGS

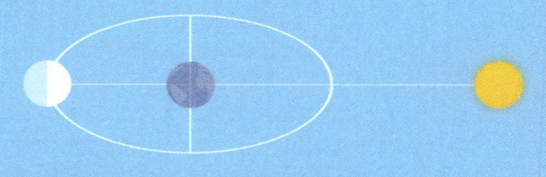

**POSITION IN ORBIT**

E 6PM → W 6AM

**MOONRISE & MOONSET**
(APPROXIMATE)

## The Full Moon happens in the middle of a lunar month

The Full Moon is undoubtedly the most exciting moon phase. It has it all; a fully illuminated face that is above the horizon from dusk till dawn, combined with the enhanced gravitational pull that creates powerful spring tides that generate exhilarating phenomena like tidal bores, whirlpools and standing waves. As long as you avoid these hazards, the Full Moon is a fantastic time for nocturnal adventures because it acts like a mirror reflecting the sun's rays onto the sea all night long (especially if the moon's declination is similar to your latitude).

Looking at the plan view of the Full Moon, you can see that it is on the opposite side of the earth to the sun. Many people logically deduce that this would make tides weaker than at the New Moon, when the moon and sun are both 'pulling' from the same direction. However, this is not the case. In fact, the moon's gravity creates forces on both sides of the earth in line with the moon, so tides at the Full Moon are equally intense as at the New Moon. Another similarity is that spring tides happen 36 hours after alignment, so the strongest tides will actually happen when there is a 'waning gibbous' moon.

# MOON PHASE
# THIRD QUARTER

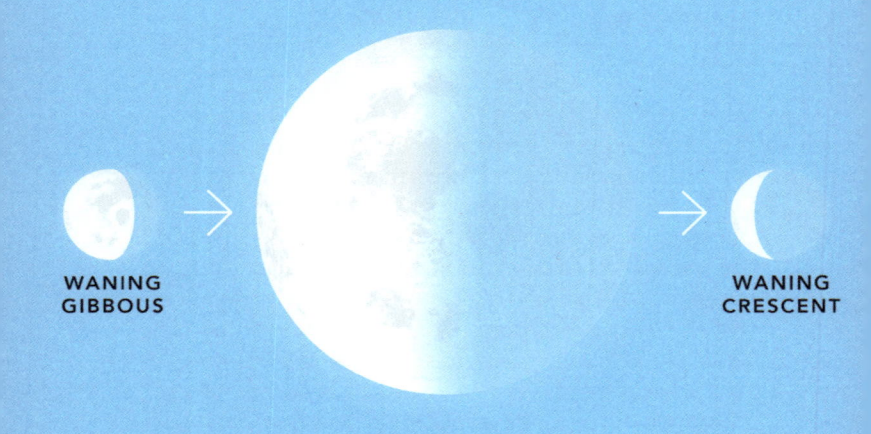

**WANING GIBBOUS** → → **WANING CRESCENT**

**TIDE INTENSITY** — MIN. NEAPS — MAX. SPRINGS

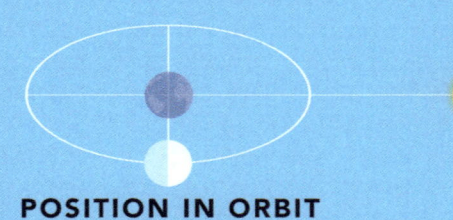

**POSITION IN ORBIT**

E — W
**MID NIGHT** — **MOONRISE & MOONSET** (APPROXIMATE) — **MID DAY**

## The Third Quarter phase happens when the left half is lit

At the Third Quarter phase, the moon has made three quarters of its monthly orbit around earth and the left side is lit up when looking from the northern hemisphere. In this respect the Third Quarter is the mirror image of the First Quarter, whose face is lit up on the right half. Their movements are opposite too; the First Quarter sets around midnight, while the Third Quarter rises around midnight. This makes the Third Quarter the perfect time for adventures that start in the pre-dawn hours because the moon will be high in the sky and guide your way before the sun rises.

This is where the differences end. When it comes to tides, things are identical at First and Third Quarters. Because they are both at right angles to the sun and earth, neap tides happen at both phases. As with springs, neaps happen 2 days after the moon phase, so expect neaps when slightly less than half the left side is illuminated (after Third Quarter) or when slightly more than the right side is lit (after First Quarter). Tide times are the same too; because high tide is 12 hours later every fortnight, if high tide is at 6 o'clock on the First Quarter it will also be 6 o'clock on the Third Quarter.

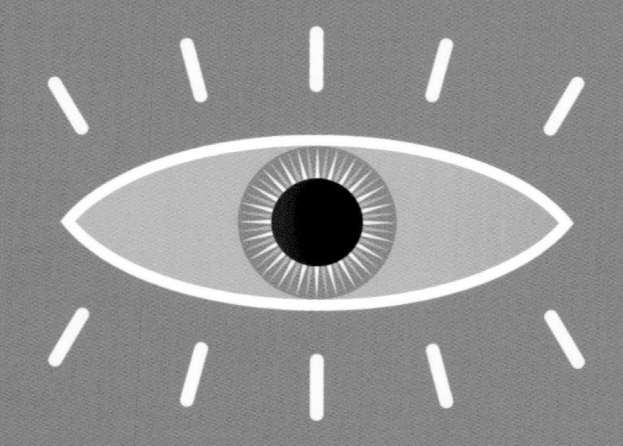

# CLUES

## FOR THE EXPLORER

By knowing the moon phase you can predict what the tides and streams are doing every hour of any day. And while looking up at this natural tide almanac as it glides through the sky you can also use it as a compass to guide you north, south, east or west.

**In this section you will learn how to navigate by the moon while using it to predict the tide times and intensity.**

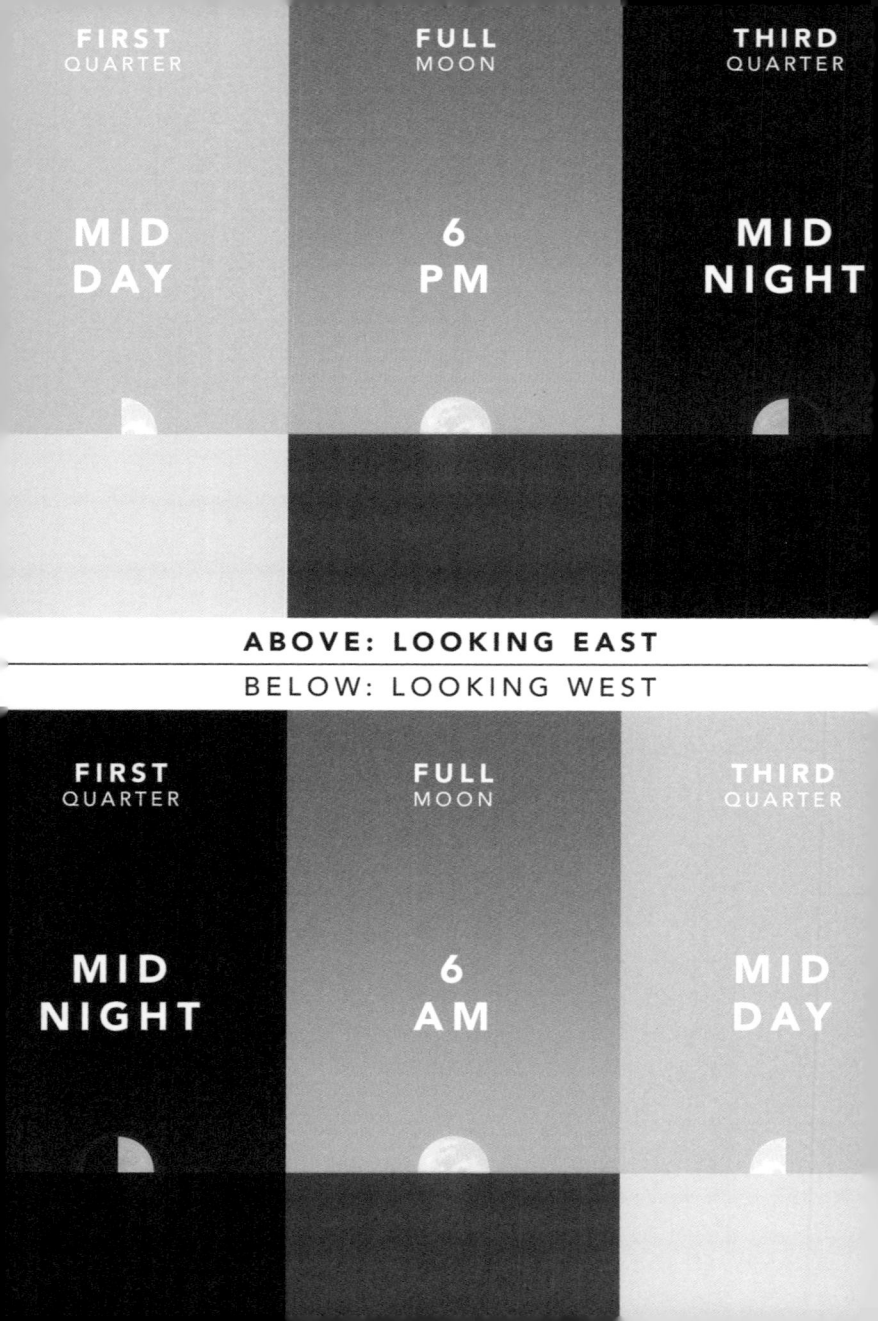

| FIRST QUARTER | FULL MOON | THIRD QUARTER |
|---|---|---|
| MID DAY | 6 PM | MID NIGHT |

**ABOVE: LOOKING EAST**

**BELOW: LOOKING WEST**

| FIRST QUARTER | FULL MOON | THIRD QUARTER |
|---|---|---|
| MID NIGHT | 6 AM | MID DAY |

## Take note of the moon on the horizon

Following the theory that celestial bodies rise in the east and set in the west, you can use this to get your bearings when you see the moon low on the horizon. With the sun the technique is easy; it rises to the east in the morning and sets to the west in the evening. But with the moon it is a little more complex because it rises and sets at different times every day. Mistaking whether it is rising or setting means you might head in the completely wrong direction, so you need to be 100% sure whether you are looking at the moonrise (east) or moonset (west) - especially if it is just a quick glance.

For example, if you see a 'half' moon in the sky at midnight, the first step is to work out if it is the First Quarter (lit on the right half when seen from the northern hemisphere) or Third Quarter (lit on the left half). Once this has been established you can quickly work out whether it is rising or setting; as you learnt with the moonlight experiment, the First Quarter phase sets around midnight, while the Third Quarter rises at the same time. So if the right half is lit up it must be setting and you will be looking west, but if the left half is illuminated then it will be rising, and you are facing east.

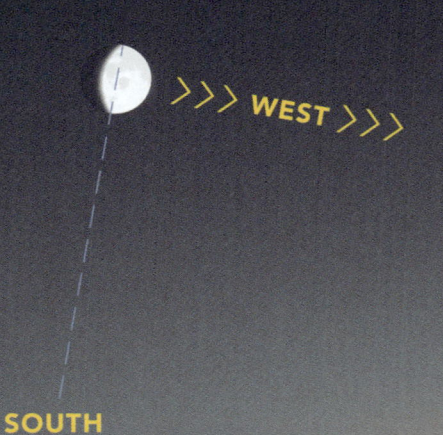

<<< EAST <<<

SOUTH

**MORNING**     **EVENING**

>>> WEST >>>

SOUTH

**Get your bearings by observing the illuminated part of the moon**

When the moon is high in the sky you can use it as a natural compass, applying a technique based on the principle that the side of the moon lit up is facing the sun (because the moon simply reflects sunlight rather than creating its own light). Therefore, if you see the Third Quarter moon in the pre-dawn hours the lit side will be facing east where the sun is below the horizon sun. In contrast, around the First Quarter phase the moon is often high in the sky after sunset so the lit face will be facing west where the sun is below the horizon.

However, you should bear in mind that lunar movements can fluctuate greatly in a short time, partly because of its proximity to earth compared to the sun and stars and also because of its tilted elliptical orbit around earth. The result is that it would be unwise to rely entirely on a single observation of the moon for navigation; instead, it should be used as a guide alongside other navigational aids. As a general rule it is sensible to look for three clues before acting on the information because one could be an anomaly – but if all three are saying the same thing, you can be confident that they are telling the truth.

**SPRINGS HAPPEN JUST AFTER FULL MOON**
WHEN A SLIVER OF THE RIGHT SIDE IS MISSING

## Gauge the tide intensity from the moon phase

By knowing the moon phase you can predict the tides. The simplest way is to gauge intensity, remembering that springs and neaps do not happen exactly on the days of the moon phases, but 36 hours after. If it is the New Moon or Full Moon today, tides will be stronger tomorrow and even more powerful the day after. But after that, they will become gradually weaker over the following week. If it is a 'half' moon today then expect neaps in 2 days time. Getting precise, if slightly less than the left half is lit or if just over half the right side is illuminated then it will be the days of neaps.

Being able to quickly spot if it is springs or neaps is an invaluable safety tool. Out on the water, the tidal streams will be much quicker during springs, so you would expect more intense whirlpools and overfalls if you were exploring places where they form (many tidal bores also only appear during springs). On dry land, it is equally useful knowing how high the tide will get because you are more likely to get cut off by the tide at springs when the water floods in faster and the tide rises higher, potentially flooding an area that remains dry at neaps.

|  | | **HW** (High Water) | **LW** (Low Water) |
|---|---|---|---|
| NEW MOON | ● **MON** | **00:00 & 12:30** | **06:00 & 18:30** |
| | TUE | 00:50 & 13:20 | 06:50 & 19:20 |
| | WED | 01:40 & 14:10 | 07:40 & 20:10 |
| | THU | 02:30 & 15:00 | 08:30 & 21:00 |
| | FRI | 03:20 & 15:50 | 09:20 & 21:50 |
| | SAT | 04:10 & 16:40 | 10:10 & 22:40 |
| | SUN | 05:00 & 17:30 | 11:00 & 21:30 |
| FIRST QUARTER | ◐ MON | 05:50 & 18:20 | 11:50 & 00:20 |
| | TUE | 06:40 & 19:10 | 12:40 & 01:10 |
| | WED | 07:30 & 20:00 | 13:30 & 02:00 |
| | THU | 08:20 & 20:50 | 14:20 & 02:50 |
| | FRI | 09:10 & 21:40 | 15:10 & 03:40 |
| | SAT | 10:00 & 22:30 | 16:00 & 04:30 |
| | SUN | 10:50 & 23:20 | 16:50 & 05:20 |
| | MON | 11:40 & 00:10 | 17:40 & 06:10 |
| FULL MOON | ○ **TUE** | **12:30** | **18:30** |

## Predict the tide times using the moon

Once you have mastered how to estimate the tide intensity from the moon phase, the next skill is to predict the tide times. To start, you need to know the time of high tide at the Full Moon, which can be done by noting the tide times on the days of several Full Moons and finding the average time to the nearest half hour to make it easy to remember. A quirk of tides is that this time will remain constant for decades, so once you have memorised the tide times for the Full Moon that knowledge can stay with you for life.

With the time of high tide for the Full Moon embedded in your memory you automatically know the tide times at the New Moon (the same) and First/Third Quarter (the opposite). This is because tides are 6 hours later every week, so if it is high tide at mid-day on the Full Moon it will be low tide around mid-day on the First and Third Quarter phases. For the days in between, simply add or subtract 50 minutes per day. To do this properly you just need to note the day of a main moon phase – for example, using the tide times opposite, if it is Thursday today and the Full Moon was on Tuesday then you would expect high tide to be around 14:10 (2 days x 50 mins. = 100 mins. after 12:30).

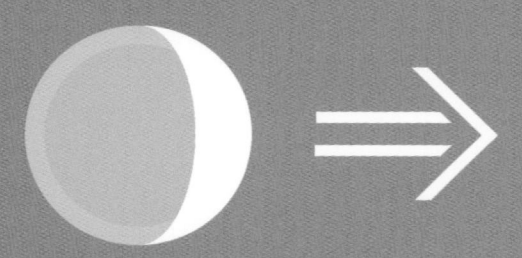

# PHENOMENA

MADE BY THE MOON

As the moon orbits the earth on its tilted elliptical orbit, a combination of variables sometimes come together at exactly the same moment to create fascinating natural phenomena like solar and lunar eclipses.

**In this section you will learn about the complex alignments that must happen simultaneously to makes rare eclipses not to be missed.**

# LUNAR
ECLIPSE

FULL
MOON

SUN

## Lunar Eclipses happen at the Full Moon

Around twice a year, a rare configuration of the moon's orbit results in the earth blocking the sun's rays from reaching the moon and somewhere on earth experiences a 'Lunar Eclipse'. For an eclipse to happen there must be two key things happening at the same moment; firstly, there must be a Full Moon with the earth directly between the moon and sun, thus blocking the light. But the reason there is not an eclipse every month is because of the second requirement, which is that the moon must be at a point on its tilted orbit so that you can draw a line through the centres of the sun, moon and earth.

When the moon has a high northerly declination, it is at the 'top' of its tilted axis and sunlight passes above earth to light the Full Moon. When it has a high southerly declination, sunlight passes below the earth to light the Full Moon. But when it has a low declination at the same time as being a Full Moon, the earth blocks the sunlight and the moon will go gradually darker to create the eclipse. But it does not disappear from sight; instead, sunlight is refracted onto the moon from our atmosphere and it creates an ominous 'blood red' appearance synonymous with a lunar eclipse.

# SOLAR ECLIPSE

NEW MOON

EARTH

## The New Moon can make a Solar Eclipse

In many respects a solar eclipse is the opposite of a lunar eclipse, happening when the moon is directly between the sun and earth to block the sun's rays from reaching our planet. On average, solar eclipses happen somewhere on earth every 18 months and they last a maximum of 7 minutes 32 seconds, but most are shorter. While it is only possible to experience a lunar eclipse at the Full Moon, solar eclipses can only happen at New Moon and it must be near perigee because this makes it appear big enough to block out the sunlight.

As a general rule, the moon must be closer than 379,300 km from earth to create a solar eclipse, which is why it cannot happen at apogee (406,700 km). Furthermore, the earth also orbits the sun on an elliptical orbit so there are times when it is further away - a time called aphelion - making the sun appear even smaller in relation to the moon; this will create even more spectacular eclipses if it coincides with perigee at exactly the same moment of a New Moon when the declination of the moon blocks the suns rays. With all these variables, it is no wonder eclipses are so rare.

A
B
C

# LUNAR DICTIONARY

**Angular Distance**
The numerical difference between your latitude and the moon's declination. For example, if your latitude is 20 degrees north and the moon's declination is 20 degrees south, the angular distance is 40 degrees (see page 22).

**Apogean Neap Tide**
A neap tide that happens when the moon is at apogee

**Apogee**
When the moon is furthest from the earth during its elliptical monthly orbit

**Celestial Body**
A 'heavenly' object - notably the sun, moon, stars and planets

**Celestial Sphere**
An imaginary sphere projecting out from earth with an equator and poles in alignment with ours. Latitudinal co-ordinates are called Declination while celestial longitude is measured as Right Ascension or Sidereal Hour Angle.

**Crescent Moon**
When less than half the moon's face is illuminated

**Culmination**
The moment a celestial body is highest in the sky each day. This happens when your meridian lines up with the sun, moon, star or planet.

## Declination
The celestial equivalent of latitude, measured up to 90 degrees north or south of the celestial equator

## Elliptical
Oval-shaped. This is the shape of the moon's orbit around earth

## Equinox
A twice-yearly event when north and south poles are equal distances from the sun

## First Quarter
A week after the New Moon, when the right half is visible from the northern hemisphere (in the southern hemisphere, the left half will be visible at the same time)

## Full Moon
When the whole of the moon's face is illuminated; the moon will be full from everywhere on earth

## Gibbous
When more than half the moon's face is illuminated

## Greenwich Meridian
An imaginary line on earth from the north pole to south pole, passing through Greenwich in the UK. Longitude is measured east or west of this meridian

### HAT / LAT
'Highest/Lowest Astronomical Tide'; the highest/lowest tide a place experiences when all astronomical factors coincide, such as a perigean spring tide at the equinox when the moon has a low declination.

### Latitude
The angular distance of a place north or south of the equator, measured up to 90 degrees

### Longitude
The angular distance of a place east or west of the Greenwich Meridian, measured up to 180 degrees

### Lunar Eclipse
A rare event when the earth blocks the sun's rays from illuminating a Full Moon

### Meridian
An imaginary line on earth from north pole to south pole, passing through your position

### Moonbow
Similar to a rainbow, but where the light comes from the moon instead of directly from the sun

### Neaps
Weak tides that happen 36 hours after the First Quarter and Third Quarter moon phases

### New Moon
The beginning of a tidal month, when the moon is directly between the sun and earth

### Noon
The moment your meridian lines up with the sun, resulting in its culmination

### Perigean Spring Tide
A powerful spring tide that happens when the moon is at perigee

### Perigee
When the moon is closest to earth on its elliptical orbit

### Sextant
An instrument for measuring the angle between two objects. This can be used to measure the altitude of the moon above the horizon for astro-navigation

### Saros
An 18-year cycle in which a series of eclipses closely repeat themselves

### Satellite
A small celestial body orbiting a planet

### Sidereal Hour Angle (SHA)
The equivalent of celestial longitude, measured in degrees westwards from the position the sun at the March equinox. Stars have a set sidereal hour angle, but the moon's SHA changes every day because it does a 360-degree orbit around the Celestial Sphere once a month

### Solar Eclipse
A rare event when a New Moon blocks the sun's rays from illuminating a place on earth

### Storm Surge
When a high astronomical tide after the New Moon or Full Moon coincides with low atmospheric pressure and onshore winds to create extra high tides that put a coastline at risk of flooding

### Syzygy
The moment two celestial bodies are in direct alignment with the sun

### Third Quarter
A week after the Full Moon, when the left half is visible from the northern hemisphere (in the southern hemisphere, the right half will be visible at the same time)

### Waning Crescent
The moon phase in between the Third Quarter and New Moon, when 25% of the left side is illuminated (when viewed from the northern hemisphere)

### Waning Gibbous
The moon phase in between the Full Moon and Third Quarter, when 75% of the left side is illuminated (when viewed from the northern hemisphere)

### Waning Moon
The period from Full Moon to New Moon when the left side is illuminated (as seen from the northern hemisphere)

### Waxing Crescent
The moon phase in between the New Moon and First Quarter, when 25% of the right side is illuminated (when viewed from the northern hemisphere)

### Waxing Gibbous
The moon phase in between First Quarter and Full Moon, when 75% of the right side is illuminated (when viewed from the northern hemisphere)

### Waxing Moon
The period from New Moon to Full Moon when the right side is illuminated (as seen from the northern hemisphere)

### Zenith
The point on the celestial sphere directly above an observer (shown by a line drawn from the centre of earth passing through your position and extending onto the celestial sphere)

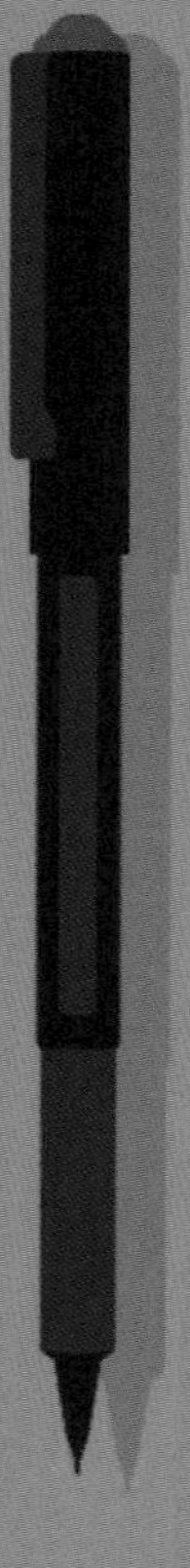

# ADVENTURE
# PLANNER

If you run out of pages or don't want to write in this book, you can download the adventure planner template and print them yourself at **www.tidalcompass.com**

Date ....................................................................

Location ..............................................................

**High Tide** __:__ (__._m) & __:__ (__._m)

Low Tide __:__ (__._m) & __:__ (__._m)

**Slack Water** __:__ & __:__ & __:__

Streams flow ____ from __:__ to __:__

Streams flow ____ from __:__ to __:__

# WIND

__:__   __:__   __:__   __:__   __:__

(N)   (N)   (N)   (N)   (N)

\_ \_   \_ \_   \_ \_   \_ \_   \_ \_
(\_ \_) (\_ \_) (\_ \_) (\_ \_) (\_ \_)

NOTES

Date ..........................................................

Location ....................................................

**High Tide** __:__ (__.__m) & __:__ (__.__m)

Low Tide __:__ (__.__m) & __:__ (__.__m)

**Slack Water** __:__ & __:__ & __:__

Streams flow ____ from __:__ to __:__

Streams flow ____ from __:__ to __:__

# WIND

__:__   __:__   __:__   __:__   __:__

- -     - -     - -     - -     - -
(_ _)   (_ _)   (_ _)   (_ _)   (_ _)

NOTES

Date .....................................................................

Location ...............................................................

**High Tide** __:__ (__.__m) & __:__ (__.__m)

Low Tide __:__ (__.__m) & __:__ (__.__m)

**Slack Water** __:__ & __:__ & __:__

Streams flow ____ from __:__ to __:__

Streams flow ____ from __:__ to __:__

# WIND

__:__   __:__   __:__   __:__   __:__

(N)   (N)   (N)   (N)   (N)

\_\_   \_\_   \_\_   \_\_   \_\_
(\_\_) (\_\_) (\_\_) (\_\_) (\_\_)

NOTES

Date ..................................................

Location ..............................................

**High Tide** __:__ (__.__m) & __:__ (__.__m)

Low Tide __:__ (__.__m) & __:__ (__.__m)

**Slack Water** __:__ & __:__ & __:__

Streams flow ____ from __:__ to __:__

Streams flow ____ from __:__ to __:__

# WIND

__:__    __:__    __:__    __:__    __:__

(N)     (N)     (N)     (N)     (N)

_ _     _ _     _ _     _ _     _ _
(_ _)   (_ _)   (_ _)   (_ _)   (_ _)

NOTES

# More books in the series...

**1 EXPLORER GUIDE**

## TIDES

AN EXPLORERS GUIDE TO TIDES

WILLIAM THOMSON

**2 EXPLORER GUIDE**

## TIDAL STREAMS

AN EXPLORERS GUIDE TO STREAMS

WILLIAM THOMSON

www.imray.com